SADLIER
FAITH AND
WITNESS

LITURGY AND WORSHIP

A Course on Prayer and Sacraments

Sr. Helen Hemmer, I.H.M.

William H. Sadlier, Inc.
9 Pine Street
New York, NY 10005-1002

Nihil Obstat
✠ Most Reverend George O. Wirz
Censor Librorum

Imprimatur
✠ Most Reverend William H. Bullock
Bishop of Madison
March 19, 1998

The *Nihil Obstat* and *Imprimatur* are official declaration that a book or pamphlet
is free of doctrinal or moral error. No implication is contained therein that
those who have granted the *Nihil Obstat* and *Imprimatur* agree with the
contents, opinions, or statements expressed.

 is a registered trademark of William H. Sadlier, Inc.

Home Office:
9 Pine Street
New York, NY 10005–1002

ISBN: 0-8215-5634-7
    456789/02 01

Contents

More Than Meets the Eye

At present we see indistinctly, as in a mirror,
but then face to face.
1 Corinthians 13:12

Reflection

I am no stranger to liturgy and worship, but I know there is more to it than meets the eye. What an opportunity I have now to get in touch with the deeper meaning of something that has been part of my life since my Baptism! Am I ready for this?

Right now, I

My prayer:
Lord Jesus, when I am praying with others in your name,
you are with me. Help me to

Symbols and rituals are part of my Catholic identity.

Symbols

Symbols are a kind of "sign language" that uncover a world of deeper meanings, ideas, and emotions. Symbols have power! I remember times when:

...the beauty of a sunset was a powerful symbol for me because

...candles and music and singing in Church were powerful symbols that reminded me of

ymbols are part of the way we communicate our belief in the sacred.

One of the most profound symbols of our Catholic faith is the space set apart for worship. It is called *sacred space*.

Some places I consider sacred space are

They are sacred to me because

y prayer:
Loving God, so many things are signs of your presence.
Open my eyes to

RITUALS are symbolic actions that often express our deepest beliefs and concerns.

Reflection

The habits and customs that make up my life
are really my personal rituals.
Seeing my life in light of symbols and rituals
can help give meaning and purpose to all that I do.

Some of my thoughts on this point:

> Rituals are at the heart of all human experiences.

My prayer:

Loving God,

When I think about my life, I realize that there are many different kinds of rituals that help me celebrate and remember who I am and what I believe.

Some family rituals that are important to me are

One important daily ritual of my faith life is

THROUGH HIM

WITH

HIM

IN

HIM

Symbols and rituals are part of my Catholic identity.

The Prayer of the Church

Lord, teach us to pray.
Luke 11:1

Lord, have I ever asked you to teach me to pray?
Is prayer important in my life?
When I think about this, I

Signs and symbols put us in touch with the divine.

Reflection

I'm beginning to realize more and more how much our Catholic worship is filled with signs and symbols and rituals. I may not understand them all, but I do know they help me to pray.

The symbol of incense reminds me

Some other signs and symbols that I find in church that help me to pray and worship are

My prayer:
I lift up my mind and heart to you, Lord.
Listen as I pray:

Liturgy is the participation of the people in the work of God.

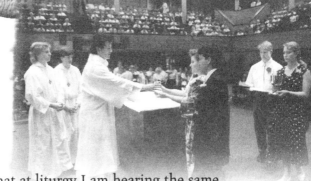

Liturgy is
the public prayer
of the Church.

flection

It is amazing to realize that at liturgy I am hearing the same
readings and praying the same psalms as the first Christians did.
Now that's *tradition!* I can see why the liturgy is the public prayer
of the Church.

Does knowing this influence how I feel about the liturgy?
Is the liturgy meaningful to me today?
I guess I would have to say

There are some aspects of the liturgy today that reflect
today's culture and traditions.
One that really helps me to pray is

y prayer:
*Loving God, I know the symbols and rituals of the Church are
full of meaning. Please help me to*

The Paschal Mystery

What makes us Catholic is our belief
in the paschal mystery of Jesus Christ.

Reflection

For over two thousand years, we have celebrated the Eucharist as
the memorial of Christ's death and resurrection.
Today, I affirm this truth when I pray these words at the Eucharis

> Christ has died,
>
> Christ is risen,
>
> Christ will come again.

Christ Jesus, I have said these words so many times.
I know they tell the story of your great love for us.
It is a story that makes me want to say

Liturgy is the participation of the people in the work of God.

Does this mean that when I participate in the liturgy,
I am participating in your work, God? Really!
What work of yours can I do?

Participating in the liturgy is more than just being there.
It means that

THROUGH HIM

WITH

HIM

IN

HIM

Liturgy is the participation of the people in the work of God.

God's Masterpieces

How great are your works, LORD!
Psalm 92:6

I only have to open my eyes to see how great are your works,
O Lord! Your marvelous plan of creation is always before me.
Hear me as I pray:

GOD'S MASTER PLAN

At the very beginning, when God created the world
and everything in it, he had a plan.

Reflection

God, your plan is very clear: If I want to know anything about
you, I have to come to know Jesus—what he did, what he said,
and who he was.

My prayer:

Jesus, you are God's plan. You are the living sign I am to follow.
Please show me

Jesus, you taught me so many things by your words and your deeds.
You taught me to

The sacraments are the celebration of our Catholic story.

The sacraments are God's masterpieces!

Reflection:
God's masterpieces! This idea really
challenges me!
The sacraments have been part of my life
since my Baptism.
Do I take them for granted? When I think
about the sacraments as God's masterpieces, I

The sacraments celebrate what we believe and live by.

Is this true for me? How have I made the sacraments part of
my faith story?

My prayer:
Lord, I really want to celebrate what I believe.
I want to celebrate that

Glory to the Father, and to the Son, and to the Holy Spirit.

ANAMNESIS · PRESENCE · DOXOLOG

EPICLESIS · BERAKAH

Reflection

These words tell the story behind the rituals and symbols of our liturgy. They help me to pray with the Church.

The prayer form called the *berakah* is a prayer of blessing. I want to pray a blessing. Here is my *berakah*:

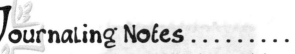

Journaling Notes . . . .

Use this space for any other thoughts you might have.

THROUGH HIM

WITH

HIM

IN

HIM

The sacraments are the celebration of our Catholic story.

The Sacrament of Sacraments

I am the living bread that came down from heaven;
whoever eats this bread will live forever; and the
bread that I will give is my flesh for the life of the world.

John 6:51

I Am the Living Bread.

Reflection

Jesus, you are with us in this sacrament of sacraments as the
Living Bread. You are really and truly present in the Eucharist
under the appearance of bread and wine.
What a wonder and mystery!

Some thoughts I have about the Eucharist:

My prayer:

Grant me, O Lord, a deeper understanding of the Eucharist
so that I

The Eucharist is the center of our lives.

> ## "Do this in memory of me."

flection

Remembering is at the heart of each of the sacraments.
At every liturgy we remember the paschal mystery: the passion, death, and resurrection of Jesus.

Jesus, I don't ever want to forget all that you have done for me.
I want to remember especially:

Holy Thursday when you

Good Friday when you

Easter Sunday when you

y prayer:

I am with you always, until the end of the age.

Matthew 28:20

Jesus, you are always with me!
What more could I ask? I don't always
remember this. But when I do, I

Reflection

I celebrate your presence in my life in a very special
way, Jesus, every time I receive you in the Eucharist.
You come to me and make me one with you.

What does all this mean for me?

We Are One Body.

We are never more the Church than when we gather around
the table of the Lord. We are the body of Christ.

How can I make myself more aware that I am part of
something much greater than myself?

My prayer:

Journaling Notes . . . .

Use this space for any other thoughts you might have.

THROUGH HIM

WITH

HIM

IN

HIM

The Eucharist is the center of our lives.

Celebrating Eucharist

Where two or three are gathered together in my name,
there am I in the midst of them.

Matthew 18:20

Gathering · Storytelling · Meal Sharing · Commissioning

The EUCHARIST

Every part of the Mass really does have a plan and a purpose.
This helps me to realize that

GATHERING

Reflection

Gathering for worship is different from any other kind of gathering.
When we gather to celebrate the Eucharist, we come together
as the Church, the body of Christ!
This is no ordinary gathering!

When I think about this I

My prayer:
Lord Jesus, help me to remember

We are the body of Christ!

STORYTELLING
Liturgy of the Word

Imagine! I am walking
with the disciples on the road to Emmaus.
I am listening to all that Jesus is saying.
I find myself longing to stay with Jesus.

Jesus, your words are powerful.
They tell me that

Jesus, help me to keep alive this longing for you.
I love you, and I want to say to you

Jesus, at every liturgy, I am given the opportunity to hear
your words again and again.

Please, give me a listening heart so that

What a privilege it must be to read the word of the Lord at Mass.
Is being a lector something I think I can do?

MEAL SHARING

During the Eucharistic prayer the priest prays:

> *May all of us who share in the body and blood*
> *of Christ*
> *be brought together in unity by the Holy Spirit.*

These words are so rich in meaning.
They remind me that

COMISSIONING

Strengthened by the Eucharist, we are commissioned:

> *"Go in peace to love and serve the Lord."*

How do I do this?

Can this make a difference in my life?

When I give my response: *"Thanks be to God"*
I am saying that

THROUGH HIM

WITH

HIM

IN

HIM

We are the body of Christ!

The Sacraments of Initiation

Baptism   Confirmation   Eucharist

I am the light of the world.

John 8:12

CONVERSION

Reflection

> *This is the time of fulfillment. The kingdom of God is at hand. Repent, and believe in the gospel.*

Mark 1:15

Jesus, keeping my life turned toward you and away from sin and selfishness is no easy task. It is especially difficult when

Jesus, when I look closely at myself today, do I see a "me first" kind of person? Is it conversion time for me?

My prayer:
Jesus, you are the light of the world.
Please

Baptism is the gateway to the Christian life.

Reflection

The Church challenges
its members to grow in faith.
Jesus, these are the ways I am
trying to grow in faith.

Instruction

Coming to know Jesus and his Church
I take this seriously because

Moral Conversion

Right and wrong behavior
This is not always easy. Sometimes it means I have to change
some things in my life because

Worship

Praying in a Catholic way by worshiping together
Jesus, how fortunate I am to belong to your Church and to be able
to share in the Eucharist. You come to me and

Ministry

Sharing faith and serving others
Jesus, I believe in you. Increase my faith. I know that you want
me to share my faith with others and so I will

When it comes to serving others, I

*The Advocate, the holy Spirit that the Father
will send in my name—he will teach you everything.*

John 14:26

CONFIRMATION

Strengthens and continues Baptism

Seals us with the Spirit

Marks us with an indelible character

Is a sign of consecration

"Be sealed with the Gift of the Holy Spirit."

Reflection

What powerful words!
Just imagine! When these words are spoken,
I am anointed and consecrated forever
to the service of Christ.

*Help me, Holy Spirit, to believe this
and show it in my life by*

My prayer:
Come, Holy Spirit,

Journaling Notes . . . .

Use this space for any other thoughts you might have.

THROUGH HIM

WITH

HIM

IN

HIM

Baptism is the gateway to the Christian life.

Our House of Prayer

Lord, I love the house where you dwell,
the tenting-place of your glory.

Psalm 26:8

The House of God

The church is the house of God. A sacred place!

Jesus, you so often sought out a place where you could pray and find strength and comfort. Sometimes you just went off by yourself to a quiet place.

When I need strength and comfort where do I go?

When I want to pray I usually

Reflection

The church is my home away from home. It's a place where I am always welcome and where you are always there for me, Jesus.

A time when I remember being in church and feeling especially close to you, Jesus, was

Lord Jesus,
Hear my prayer today that

The parish church is a visible witness to the presence of Christ.

Behold, God's dwelling is with the human race.
He will dwell with them and they will be his people
and God himself will always be with them.

Revelation 21:3

Reflection

No wonder the tabernacle is always so beautiful and always
in a special place of honor in the church! The tabernacle is
the dwelling place of Jesus, who is really and truly present
in the Blessed Sacrament.

Catholics have a long tradition of praying
before the Blessed Sacrament.

My prayer:

Jesus, present in the Blessed Sacrament, here are some things I want
to say to you:

In church a candle always burns before the tabernacle when the
Blessed Sacrament is present. The burning candle reminds me

TRUE BEAUTY

Reflection

The true beauty of the parish church is not found in its architecture but rather in the hospitality of the parishioners, their devotion to the Eucharist, and their love and service of others.

As a member of my parish how am I contributing to its life and beauty?

Hospitality

Lord Jesus, there are many ways I show hospitality, but the one I do best is

Devotion to the Eucharist

Jesus, I love you. When I think about your presence in the Eucharist, I

Love and Service of Others

Lord Jesus, you tell me to love my neighbor as myself. You know it is not easy to do, but I

Some things about my parish church that help me to pray and worship are:

Journaling Notes . . . .

Use this space for any other thoughts you might have.

THROUGH HIM

WITH

HIM

IN

HIM

The parish church is a visible witness to the presence of Christ.

CHAPTER 8

Seasons of Praise

Every day I will bless you;
I will praise your name forever.

Psalm 145:2

Lord, are the words of this psalm true in my life?
In what ways?

SUNDAY...

...is the original
Christian feast day.

THE LORD'S DAY

Reflection

Gathering for Eucharist is at the very heart of the meaning of
Sunday. Is this just an obligation for me, or is it something more?

My prayer:

Sunday is the key to the whole liturgical year.

Unless a grain of wheat falls to the ground and dies, it remains just a grain of wheat; but if it dies, it produces much fruit.

John 12:24

prayer • fasting • almsgiving

LENT

Reflection

Lent is about **"letting go"** and **"moving on."**
Am I like the grain of wheat? Am I ready to let go and move on to grow in my faith?

What things in my life do I need to let go of this Lent?
How should I begin?

Celebrating THE TRIDUUM

Reflection

The liturgies of the Triduum are filled with rituals
and symbols that help us enter into the meaning
of Christ's life, death, and resurrection.
These days are the most important of the Church year.

Jesus,

...will you find me at the table of the Eucharist on Holy Thursday evening?
...will you find me kneeling at the foot of the cross on Good Friday?
...will you find me holding the burning candle and singing alleluia
on Easter?

My prayer:

Jesus,

Darkness
Light

Fire
Water

Walking
Standing
Kneeling

Jesus, the symbols of the Triduum speak to me about what you
have done for me. They tell me that

Journaling Notes . . . .

Use this space for any other thoughts you might have.

THROUGH HIM

WITH

HIM

IN

HIM

Sunday is the key to the whole liturgical year.

CHAPTER 9

A Year of Glory

*The LORD's love for us is strong;
the LORD is faithful forever.*

Psalm 117:2

Lord, your love for us is so great! so strong!
Help me never to forget this, especially when

EASTER The Challenge of the great fifty days of Easter is to continue Christ's life in the world.

Reflection

In Baptism I "put on Christ". I am part of his body, the Church.
How do I continue his life in my world today...

...as a healthy person

...as a forgiving person

...as a serving person

My prayer:

The Holy Spirit is given to every Christian, to all who believe.

The Message of Pentecost

As the Father has sent me, so I send you.

John 20:21

The message is loud and clear! We are to continue the mission of Jesus. The seven gifts of the Holy Spirit equip us for this mission.

WISDOM • COURAGE • REVERENCE • UNDERSTANDING

RIGHT JUDGMENT • KNOWLEDGE • WONDER AND AWE

Jesus, help me to believe in the power of the Holy Spirit in my life. Jesus, listen to my prayer for the gift of the Spirit that I most need now:

"There is a season, turn, turn, turn. . .
And a time for every purpose under heaven."

The fifty-day season of Easter is a special time for me to turn to
meditation on the gospels,
sharing in the Eucharist,
and doing good works.

When it comes to meditating on the gospels, I

Sharing in the Eucharist is

As for doing good works, I

My prayer:

CHRISTMAS

Christmas teaches us to live in the present.
Christ comes now.

Reflection

It is in the present that we find Jesus, not yesterday,
not tomorrow, but today.

My prayer:

Lord, increase my faith! Help me to recognize your presence
in my life each day so that I

ORDINARY TIME

Our Christian life is not just Christmas and Easter.
It is also all the days in between, called Ordinary
Time.

Reflection

The truly valuable things in our lives are achieved
little by little, day after day.

The valuable things in life!

Is coming to know more about the life and works of Jesus
something I value? How do I show it?

My prayer:

Journaling Notes . . . .

Use this space for any other thoughts you might have.

THROUGH HIM

WITH

HIM

IN

HIM

The Holy Spirit is given to every Christian, to all who believe.

CHAPTER 10

The Sacrament of Reconciliation

"Lord, you are kind and forgiving,
most loving to all who call on you.".

Psalm 86:5

Lord, do you see me as a kind and forgiving person? Am I a loving person to all who call on me? I know in my heart

Reflection

The sacrament of Reconciliation celebrates our continuing conversion, our turning from selfishness and sin to the spirit of love and generosity.

I know I need to turn from selfishness and sin. Do I turn to this sacrament for the grace and help I need to do this? How often?

My prayer:

All-loving God, I praise you for your great love for me. Increase my desire to

Forgiveness of sins is central to the message of Jesus.

A RECONCILING CHURCH

Reflection

The greatest evil we can have in our lives is sin.

The greatest gift we can receive is God's love and forgiveness.

Forgiveness • Conversion • Reconciliation

Are these just words that I hear or read about, or do they have real meaning in my life?

When I think about forgiveness, I

When I think about conversion, I

When I think about reconciliation, I

In the gospels forgiveness of sins is central to the message of Jesus. Can I recall a time in the gospels when Jesus assures us that forgiveness is always there for us if we ask for it?

My prayer:

Conversion of Heart

The sacrament of Reconciliation keeps us on track in our own individual work of conversion.

This picture reminds me that one of the most important ways I keep on track is

Conversion is a grace of the Holy Spirit. Conversion is the work of a lifetime!

Holy Spirit, be my guide and my strength each day so that I

Conversion is about honestly admitting my faults.

Holy Spirit, help me to be honest with myself so that I

Conversion is about having the courage to strive to do better.

Holy Spirit, increase my desire and my courage to

ournaling Notes . . . .

THROUGH HIM

WITH

HIM

IN

HIM

Forgiveness of sins is central to the message of Jesus.

CHAPTER 11

The Anointing of the Sick

*He cured many who were sick with various
diseases, and he drove out many demons.*

Mark 1:34

Jesus And Healing

Reflection

On almost every page of the gospels, we see Jesus bringing health
and wholeness to those who are ill and suffering.

A gospel account about healing that is especially meaningful to me
is the story of

This account helps me to

When was the last time I prayed for someone
who was seriously ill?
Was it a family member or friend?

Jesus, I know I can help those who are sick and suffering this day by
my prayers. Listen, as I pray:

*In this sacrament we pray that the sick will be healed
in body, in soul, and in spirit.*

Celebration of Anointing

Jesus told his disciples to continue his work of healing the sick.
"So . . . they anointed with oil many who were sick
and cured them."

Mark 6:12–13

Reflection

The Church continues this ministry in many ways today and
celebrates it in the sacrament of the Anointing of the Sick.

Imagine
for a moment . . . .

I have come to help in the celebration of this sacrament in my
parish. Jesus, you are always with us.
Jesus, at this special time I think you would say

Jesus, you often comforted the sick. Today, I think you would

My prayer:

Healing and Anointing

Reflection

The oil used in this sacrament is blessed by the bishop on Holy Thursday. It is this blessing that makes the oil sacramental.

When the bishop blesses the oil he says:

Make this oil a remedy for all who are anointed
with it;
heal them in body, in soul, and in spirit,
and deliver them from every affliction.

What powerful words of blessing! What a beautiful prayer!
Is there someone I would like to ask God to heal right now?

My prayer:
Loving and healing God, I have something I want ot ask you…

Journaling Notes . . . .

Use this space for any other thoughts you might have.

THROUGH HIM

WITH

HIM

IN

HIM

In this sacrament we pray that the sick will be healed
in body, in soul, and in spirit.

CHAPTER 12

The Sacrament of Holy Orders

*Thus should one regard us:
as servants of Christ and as stewards
of the mysteries of God.*

1 Cor:inthians 4:1

Bishops

Reflection

These are some of the words from the Prayer of Consecration of bishops:

> *Father, you know all hearts.
> You have chosen your servant for the office of bishop.
> May he be a shepherd to your holy flock,
> and a high priest blameless in your sight,
> ministering to you night and day;
> may he always gain the blessing of your favor
> and offer the gifts of your holy Church.*

*Loving God, this prayer of the Church for bishops helps me
to remember that*

What words would I like to add as my prayer for the bishop of
my diocese?

The priesthood is essential to the life of the Church.

There is only one priesthood, the priesthood of Christ.

The Priesthood of Christ

These are some of the words from the Prayer of Consecration of priests:

> Almighty Father,
> grant to these servants of yours
> the dignity of the priesthood.
> Renew within them the Spirit of holiness.
> As co-workers with the order of bishops
> may they be faithful to the ministry
> that they receive from you, Lord God,
> and be to others a model of right conduct.

Loving God, this prayer for priests helps me to remember that

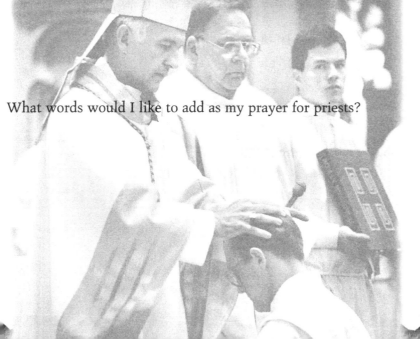

What words would I like to add as my prayer for priests?

Deacons ordained for service

As a newly ordained minister, the deacon kneels before the bishop and receives the Book of the Gospels. The bishop says to him:

Receive the Gospel of Christ
whose herald you now are.
Believe what you read,
teach what you believe,
and practice what you teach.

This prayer for deacons tells me three things:

Believe what you read.
I can do this when

Teach what you believe.
I can do this when

Practice what you teach.
I can do this when

Stephen, patron saints of deacons, pray for all deacons and for us.

Journaling Notes . . . .

Use this space for any other thoughts you might have.

THROUGH HIM

WITH

HIM

IN

HIM

The priesthood is essential to the life of the Church.

CHAPTER 13

The Sacrament of Matrimony

What God has joined together,
no human being must separate.
Matthew 19:6

Reflection

As ministers of the sacrament to each other,
the couple exchange vows by saying:

> *"I promise to be true to you in good times and in bad,*
> *in sickness and in health. I will love you and honor you*
> *all the days of my life."*

All the days of my life! This is a promise! This is a vow!
The sacrament of Matrimony is a commitment for life!

Lord God, I know that making promises and keeping promises
are two different things.

Am I a person who keeps my promises, even difficult ones?

Have I made a promise lately that is a challenge for me to keep?

My prayer:
Lord Jesus, being a person of my word is

The sacrament of Matrimony is a life-giving sign of grace.

God is love, and whoever remains in love, remains in God.

1 John 4:16

reparing for Marriage

Taking time to prepare for important things in life is not just a good idea. It is absolutely necessary if I want to succeed.

When did I last take time to prepare for something important? How did I feel about doing that? Did I ask for God's help?

eflection

Matrimony is a sacrament. Therefore it requires special preparation through prayer and reflection.

When I think about this sacrament, I pray that

elebrating Matrimony

In one of the blessings at the end of the wedding liturgy, the priest prays:

> *that the peace of Christ may always be in the couple's home*
> *that they will live in peace with all people*
> *that they will always bear witness to the love of God in the world.*

ly prayer:

Loving God, may this prayer of blessing be upon every couple and every home. I ask especially for your blessing upon

Reflection
What kind of a person do I want to be? What kind of a person am I becoming?

My Interpersonal Skills

Am I a good listener? How do I show this?

How do I deal with criticism?

What is my reaction when my plans are upset for some reason?

Do I apologize when I've made a mistake or caused a problem?

What do I do when I am angry? How do I solve the problem?

Do I speak with adults respectfully and courteously?

Do I give positive feedback? Do I affirm others and thank them when I am grateful for their help or support?

Do I look for ways to help others when I can?

If I have a serious problem or need, do I talk it over with an adult I can tr

My prayer:
Dear God, help me to be open and honest with you and with myself.

THROUGH HIM

WITH

HIM

IN

HIM

The sacrament of Matrimony is a life-giving sign of grace.

CHAPTER 14

Mary and the Saints

*You are fellow citizens with the holy ones
and members of the household of God.*

Ephesians 2:19

COMMUNION OF SAINTS

I am a member of the household of God.
I belong to the communion of saints.

Lord, just knowing that I am not alone in my struggle to follow
you helps me to

Reflection

Just think! The saints in heaven help me by their prayers!
Even the saints pray!

Am I faithful to prayer? Do I make sure that prayer is part
of my life every day?
When are my special times of prayer?

I know the names and stories of many saints, but there is one saint
who is very special to me:
This saint is special because

We honor the saints because they show us how to follow Christ.

A RICH TRADITION

> Holiness is achieved, not by doing great things,
> but by allowing God's greatness to work in us.

Reflection

Millions of people have lived holy lives and are saints.
But not all saint are canonized.
This makes me think

I am called to a life of holiness. I am called to be a saint.

What does this mean for me today?

My prayer:

Lord Jesus, work in me. Help me to be holy.
Help me to learn from Mary and the saints to

MARY is the first of the disciples and the model for all Christians.

Reflection

Mary is the mother of Jesus

> Mary, you are my mother, too.
> Mary, hear me as I pray:

Mary is the first disciple of Jesus.

> Mary, I am a disciple of Jesus, too.
> Mary, hear me as I pray:

Hail Mary, full of grace,
the Lord is with you!
Blessed are you among women,
and blessed is the fruit of your womb, Jesus.
Holy Mary, Mother of God
Pray for us sinners,
now and at the hour of our death.
Amen.

Mary, today I pray this petition to you with all my heart:

> Holy Mary, Mother of God,
> pray for us sinners,
> now and at the hour of our death.
> Amen

Journaling Notes . . . .

Use this space for any other thoughts you might have.

THROUGH HIM

WITH

HIM

IN

HIM

We honor the saints because they show us how to follow Christ.

CHAPTER 15

Paths of Prayer

Pray always without becoming weary.

Luke 18:1

Paths don't just happen. They are made, usually by people trying to find their way.

Prayer doesn't just happen. Praying makes prayer happen. How am I making prayer paths for myself?

PRAYER PATHS

Thanksgiving We thank God for his gifts.
I thank you, God, today especially for

Contrition We express sorrow for sin.
I am sorry, God, for

Petition We pray for others.
I want to pray in a special way for

Adoration We praise him for his goodness.
I praise you, God, with all my heart for

The Our Father

The most perfect of prayers

Lord, teach me to pray.
And Jesus said, "This is how you are to pray:"

Our Father,

who art in heaven, hallowed be thy name;
thy kingdom come; thy will be done on earth as it is in heaven.
Give us this day our daily bread; and forgive us our trespasses
as we forgive those who trespass against us;
and lead us not into temptation,
but deliver us from evil.
Amen.

Reflection

Jesus, I have prayed the Our Father many times. The words of your prayer that challenge me are

Jesus, the words of the Our Father that I especially want to remember and pray this week are

Jesus, help me to live the real meaning of the Our Father in my daily life.

Praying with Scripture

Reflection

Peace I leave with you; my peace I give to you.
Not as the world gives do I give it to you.
Do not let your hearts be troubled or afraid.

John 14:27

Jesus, *these words of yours tell me that*

Reflection

And I tell you, ask and you will receive;
seek and you will find;
knock and the door will be opened to you.

Luke 11:9

Jesus, *you make it very clear that*

My closing prayer:

Jesus, *you have told me many other things. The one that has helped me the most is*

Journaling Notes . . . .

Use this space for any other thoughts you might have.

THROUGH HIM

WITH

HIM

IN

HIM

Jesus, help me to live the real meaning
of the Our Father in my daily life.

Acknowledgments

Scripture selections taken from the *New American Bible*
Copyright © 1991, 1986, 1970 by the Confraternity of Christian
Doctrine, Washington, D.C. and are used by license of the
copyright owner. All rights reserved. No part of the
New American Bible may be used or reproduced in any form,
without permission in writing from the copyright owner.

English Translation of Ordination of Deacons, Priests and Bishops @ 1975,
International Committee on English in the Liturgy, Inc. (ICEL)

Photo Credits

Photo Editor
Jim Saylor

Associate Photo Editor
Lori Berkowitz

Karen Callaway: 49.
Myrleen Cate: 42.
Comstock: 25.
Crosiers/ Gene Plaisted, OSC: 9, 13 both, 16, 18, 21, 26 both, 30, 46, 52.
FPG/ Barbara Peacock: 33; Miguel Sanchez: 53, Ron Thomas: 60.
The Granger Collection: 44.
Anne Hamersky: 8.
The Image Bank/ Harold Sund: 5; Anthony A. Buccaccio: 28; Michael Melford
57.
Ken Karp: 4, 22 both.
Chris Sheridan: 14, 45, 48.
Larry Ulrich: 36.
Bill Wittman: 20, 29, 32, 40.